POINTS
OF
REBELLION

POINTS
OF
REBELLION

———————

WILLIAM O.
DOUGLAS

VINTAGE BOOKS
A Division of Random House
New York

CONTENTS

I

How America
Views
Dissent

The continuing episodes of protest and dissent in the United States have their basis in the First Amendment to the Constitution, a great safety valve that is lacking in most other nations of the world. The First Amendment creates a sanctuary around the citizen's beliefs. His ideas, his conscience, his convictions are his own concern, not the government's.

After an American has been in a totalitarian country for several months, he is greatly relieved when he reaches home. He feels that bonds have been released and that he is free. He can speak above a whisper, and he walks relaxed and unguarded as though he were no longer being followed. After a recent trip I said to a neighbor, "It's wonderful to be back in a nation where even a riot may be tolerated."

All dissenters are protected by the First Amendment. A "communist" can be prosecuted

for actions against society, but not for express-
ing his views as to what the world order should
be. Although television and radio time as well
as newspaper space is available to the affluent
members of this society to disseminate their
views, most people cannot afford that space.
Hence, the means of protest, and the customary
manner of dissent in America, from the days of
the American Revolution, has been pamphleteering.

Other methods of expression, however, are
also protected by the First Amendment—from
picketing, to marching on the city streets, to
walking to the State Capital or to Congress, to
assembling in parks and the like.

It was historically the practice of state police
to use such labels as "breach of the peace" or
"disorderly conduct" to break up groups of minorities who were protesting in these unorthodox
ways. The real crime of the dissenters was that
they were out of favor with the Establishment,
and breach of the peace or disorderly conduct
was used merely as a cloak to conceal the true
nature of the prosecution.

In 1931 the Supreme Court, in an opinion by

Chief Justice Charles Evans Hughes, held that the First Amendment was applicable to the States by reason of the Due Process Clause of the Fourteenth Amendment. That Clause provides that no State shall deny any person "liberty" without "due process." The Hughes Court held that the right to dissent, protest, and march for that purpose was within the purview of the First Amendment. Breach of the peace and disorderly conduct could, therefore, no longer be used as an excuse for the prosecution of minorities.

Parades, of course, can be regulated to avoid traffic problems and to allow for easy access to public offices by other people. Pickets may be regulated as to numbers and times and places. But the basic right of public protest may not be abridged.

While violence is not protected by the Constitution, lawful conduct, such as marching and picketing, often boils over into unlawful conduct because people are emotional, not rational, beings. So are the police; and very often they arrest the wrong people. For the police are an arm of the Establishment and view protesters with suspicion. Yet American protesters need not be submissive. A speaker who resists arrest is acting as a free man. The police do not have *carte blanche* to interfere with his freedom. They do not have the license to arrest at will or to silence people at will.

This is one of the many instances showing how the Constitution was designed to keep government off the backs of the people.

Our Constitutional right to protest allows us more freedom than most other people in the world enjoy. Yet the stresses and strains in our system have become so great and the dissents so violent and continuous that a great sense of insecurity has possessed much of the country.

This insecurity reflects international as well as local worries and concerns. At the international level we have become virtually paranoid. The world is filled with dangerous people. Every troublemaker across the globe is a communist. Our obsession is in part the product of a fear generated by Joseph McCarthy. Indeed a black silence of fear possesses the nation and is causing us to jettison some of our libertarian traditions.

Truman nurtured that fear. Johnson promoted it, preaching the doctrine that the people of the world want what we have and, unless suppressed, will take it from us. That fear has made us all military experts—we all know what missiles to keep, what troop deployments to make, what overseas wars to search out and join. Military strategy has indeed become dominant in our thinking; and the dominance of the military attitude has had a sad effect at home.

Domestic issues also have aroused people as seldom before. The release of the Blacks from the residual institutions of slavery has filled many white communities with fear; and the backlash has had profound political consequences.

The affluent society with its marketing mechanisms and its vivid television commercials has whetted the appetites of the poorest of the poor for the good things of the material world.

The spreading awareness of the impoverished conditions of humanity across the globe, and of the needless deprivations of the masses, has stirred even the illiterates to action.

There have always been grievances and youth has always been the agitator. Why then is today different? Why does dissent loom so ominously? Some attribute the current regime of dissent to provocateurs inspired by foreign interest. The Soviets are accused by some; Peking is blamed by others. Yet, there can be no doubt that ideas of revolution have long been loose in the world. The concepts behind our revolution of 1776 spread overseas and greatly bothered more people than those who wore crowns. The French revolution of 1789 and its ideas of liberty, equality, and the right to resist oppression shook up the Establishment of that age. The Declaration of the Rights of Man and the Citizen, August 26, 1789, became the creed of several European nations.

The theories of Marx and Lenin had an even greater world impact because of the arrival of the age of communications. And the Maoist Chinese, with their very special competence in propaganda, have greatly exploited the weaknesses both in developing nations and in affluent societies.

But the fact that communists may have provoked some of the present dissent in the United States is not, as some would have it, the end of the matter. The voices are not communist, for those in rebellion see communism as an even more vicious form of a status quo. The merits must be voted up or voted down. For there is no doubt that the elements of discord in our lives reveal major issues that are causing a serious domestic dislocation.

Forces too numerous to catalogue have produced a decade of protests that is in many ways unique:

Uniqueness of Protests

(1) It comes during a time of prolonged affluence, not of depression;

(2) It is not ideological in its orientation, but is essentially activist;

(3) It is led by the young people who, though not unanimous in tactics or in objectives, have given these protests a revolutionary tone. The goal of their revolution is not to destroy the regime of technology. It is to make the existing system more human, to make the machine subservient to man, to allow for the flowering of a society where all the idiosyncracies of man can be honored and respected.

Older people are not receptive to these protests nor do they understand them. The older generation might well have resisted all change in any case, but they are doomed to resist because of the conditioning they have experienced over the last few decades.

I speak now of two forces working to that end. First is the growing subservience of man to the machine. Man has come to realize that if he is to have material "success," he must honor the folklore of the corporation state, respect its desires, and walk to the measure of its thinking. The interests of the corporation state are to convert all the riches of the earth into dollars. Its techniques, fashioned mainly on Madison Avenue and followed in Washington, D. C., are to produce climates of conformity that make any competing idea practically un-American. The older generation has in the main become mindless when it comes to criticism of the system. For it, perpetuation of the corporation state and its glorification represent the true Americanism. "If only the world were like us, everything would be perfect."

The second force which is shaping resistance

to change is the way in which our First Amendment traditions have been watered down or discarded altogether.

The First Amendment was designed so as to permit a flowering of man and his idiosyncracies, but we have greatly diluted it. Although the Amendment says that Congress shall make "no law" abridging freedom of speech and press, this has been construed to mean that Congress may make "some laws" that abridge that freedom.

The courts have written some astonishing decisions in that area. Here are a few examples:

A person may not be punished for believing a so-called noxious or communist doctrine; but he may be punished for being an "active" advocate of that ideology.

A person may not be prosecuted for reading or teaching Karl Marx; but he may be sent to prison for "conspiring" with others to conduct classes or seminars on the Marxist creed.

A person may be convicted for making a speech or for pamphleteering if a judge rules *ex post facto* that the speaker or publisher created a "clear and present danger" that his forbidden or revolutionary thesis would be accepted by at least some of the audience.

A person may be convicted of publishing a book if the highest Court, in time, decides that the book has no "socially redeeming value."

In these and in many other respects we have fostered a climate of conformity.

In O'Henry Junior High School, Austin, Texas, some thirteen-year-old boys were threatened with expulsion for getting out a home-mimeographed paper calling for an end to compulsory daily prayers over the public address system, which practice is, of course, contrary to the Court's ruling in *Engle v. Vitale,* 370 U. S. 421. One boy was actually called an atheist and a communist because he maintained that the requirement of compulsory prayers was teaching the pupils to break the law of the land.

Throughout the country the climate within our public schools has been against the full flowering of First Amendment traditions.

The great rewards are in the Establishment and in work for the Establishment. While the Establishment welcomes inventive genius at the scientific level (provided it can get the patent and lock it up against competitive use), it does not welcome dissent on the great racial, ideological, and social issues that face our people.

Our colleges and universities reflect primarily the interests of the Establishment and the status quo. Heavy infiltration of CIA funds has stilled critical thought in some areas. The use of Pentagon funds for classified research has developed enclaves within our universities for favored professors, excluding research participation by students. The Pentagon now has, for example, contracts with forty-eight universities for research on how to make birds useful in aerial photography, gunnery, steering of missiles, detection of mines, and search-and-destroy operations.

The University of California has been up to its ears in research on nuclear explosives with huge grants from the Atomic Energy Commission. MIT and Johns Hopkins—in terms of the dollar volume of their contracts—have been among the hundred major military-aerospace corporations. Stanford, Columbia, and Michigan have been rich with defense contracts. And so the list grows.

Only revolutionary-minded faculties would

provide a curriculum relevant to either domestic or foreign political problems. Very few faculty members have a revolutionary fervor or insight.

Our private universities are self-perpetuating. As Kenneth Galbraith has said, the trustees are drawn from such a "narrow spectrum of social and political opinion" as to make them insensitive to issues of the real world. Even their faculties are subordinate to the orthodoxy of the trustees and the students have little voice in affairs that vitally affect their interests. For example, much of modern education fills young, tender minds with information that is utterly irrelevant to modern problems of the nation or to the critical conditions of the world. Students rightfully protest; and while all of their complaints do not have merit, they too should be heard, as of right, and not be compelled to resort to violence to obtain a hearing.

The university—symbol of the Establishment —is used to having its way in a community. Its pressure is commonly applied to Black areas; as it needs to expand, Black tenements provide an easy target. The university action that triggers a violent reaction from the Black community may also be of a different kind. Morningside Park in New York City has long been a rather rugged green belt between Columbia University and Harlem. It was indeed one of Harlem's few escapes—to shade, playground, and recreation. When Columbia started to build its gymnasium there, many of us in the conservation field were up in arms. But none of us had the personal stake in that piece of woods that the people of Harlem had. And it was they who rebelled and joined the ominous confrontation at Columbia.

But the case against the university is that it is chiefly a handmaiden of the state or of industry or, worse yet, of the military-industrial complex. In this connection Dr. Robert M. Hutchins recently stated:

It seems probable that we are entering a postindustrial age in which the issue is not how to produce or even distribute goods, but how to live human lives, not how to strengthen and enrich the nation state, but how to make the world a decent habitation for mankind. The causes of the present unrest among students are of course very complicated, but one of them is a feeling among young people that contemporary institutions, and particularly the university, cannot in their present form deal with the dangers and opportunities of the coming age.

The dangers are obvious enough, and the opportunities, though less often referred to, are equally great. The chance is there to have what Julian Huxley has called the 'fulfillment society' and what others have called the learning society, or simply a human society. We have no very clear conception of what such a society would be like. But we have all learned from *1984* and *Brave New World* what some other possibilities are.

When the university does not sit apart, critical of industry, the Pentagon, and government, there is no fermentative force at work in our society. The university becomes a collection of technicians in a service station, trying to turn out better technocrats for the technological society. Then all voices become a chorus supporting the status quo; there is no challenger from the opposition warning of dangers to come. The result is a form of goose-stepping and the installation of conformity as king. Such has been the increasing tendency in this country for the last quarter century.

Our search for the ideological stray, through loyalty and security hearings, has vastly accelerated our trend to conformity.

Anyone who works for the federal or for any state government must run the gauntlet. Everyone who works for contractors or subcontractors on defense work must also be cleared. We have run at least twenty million people through those security hearings since Truman established the tests in 1947. The casualties have been staggering in the past and they continue to mount. People have been disqualified for governmental work particularly during the McCarthy days, because they:

— opposed our support of the French in Vietnam.

— attended a social gathering sponsored by a group that turned out to be "subversive."

— predicted the fall of Chiang Kai-Shek in China and the victory of the Communists.

The hearings seldom dealt with overt acts against the United States. They probed thoughts, attitudes, and beliefs. At various times a man was suspect—and often suspended—if he believed in the U. N., if he thought schools should be segregated, if he thought Peking should be admitted to the U. N.

Our loyalty and security boards developed many "badges" that marked a "subversive" employee, or one who was a poor "security risk."

"Do you own Paul Robeson records?"

"Do you own any works of Picasso or Matisse?"

"Did you vote for Henry Wallace?"

"Have you ever studied the Russian language?"

Thousands lost their jobs because of these trivia. Others were suspended and turned into the outer darkness because of their membership in organizations deemed "subversive." The organization may or may not have had Communist members; the employee's association with it may have been only nominal or fleeting. I remember one file of an honored Negro in the Seattle community who lost his job because he innocently attended a "coffee hour" of one such organization.

Membership in the Communist Party was of course fatal even though those memberships, at least in the early years, were often not "knowing" associations with the aim of overthrowing the government.

Apart from the improper use of data which are highly subjective and not subject to refutation by the victim, there are some data which are of no concern to government. All branches of the government are bound by the Bill of Rights. It is of no concern to government what a person believes, what he thinks, what philosophy he embraces.

— "What church do you belong to?"

— "Are you an atheist?"

— "What are your views on the United Nations?"

These and like inquiries are irrelevant.

A man's belief is his own; he is the keeper of his conscience; Big Brother has no rightful concern in these areas.

There never was an end to these investigations. Hearings followed hearings, as each succeeding administrator hoped to trap an employee, label him a "subversive," and add to the administrator's popular image. This shabby business was illustrated by the pursuit of John Paton Davies, our foremost China expert in

the forties and fifties. He was cleared by eight
loyalty-security boards. Then, in 1954, he was
tried the ninth time and dismissed from the
Foreign Service by John Foster Dulles. In 1968
he was "tried" for the tenth time and this time
given a security clearance.

In the sixties employees were still being
screened for association with so-called communist "front" organizations, not especially
present associations but associations dating way
in the past when friendship with Russia, welded
in World War II, was considered a national vir-
tue. In the sixties, even association with the
Civil Liberties Union was considered by some
hearing officers as a badge of a poor security
risk.

These hearings have had a powerful leveling
effect; they indeed have resulted in a bureaucracy more staid, more conservative, and more
timid than a nation can afford in a revolutionary
world.

The growing dossiers on people, in employment files and in security files, have been a paral-
lel phenomenon. Age, income, place of birth,
education are innocuous points of information.

But much of the data in present personnel files is highly subjective. Is the applicant "reliable," "cooperative," "stable," "loyal," or "subversive?" has been asked of former teachers, associates, or employers. The answers may reflect an emotional rift between the applicant and the person being interviewed. The latter may be "rightist," the applicant "leftist." The answer may reflect an old grudge or a casual episode that has no present significance. Yet the applicant has no chance to see the report, to challenge it, or to have it corrected.

The data collected on an applicant may reflect one youthful transgression that never was repeated. One private group, keeping tabs on people who join demonstrations or march in protests, has files covering five million or more, available for a fee.

An ominous trend is the increasing FBI activity on present-day college and university campuses. They put under complete surveillance a member or leader of the Students for a Democratic Society group (SDS), monitoring every minute of months of his life. The following message from an educator with administra-

POINTS OF
REBELLION

tive responsibilities on the Atlantic seaboard tells the story in a nutshell, though the FBI will deny it:

> I want to reiterate my concern about the activities of the Federal Bureau of Investigation on college campuses. Your help in stopping what most Americans would consider to be invasion of privacy and the beginnings of a police state is solicited.
>
> In addition to the usual investigative procedures for security clearances in criminal cases, the FBI has been conducting field checks on individual students and faculty members who are suspected of being members of 'activist' groups. What it has come to mean is that any faculty member or student who speaks out or attends meetings of such groups (e.g., SDS) is apt to be investigated.
>
> It is not unusual for the FBI to 'plant' a student in such groups as SDS and reimburse the student for his information. Furthermore, leaders of these organizations are placed under a system of national surveillance.
>
> These 'spy' activities have also moved to other levels of police activity. At our local State Police barracks, for example, there are files, including pictures, of members of SDS.
>
> I include myself among those who consider

SDS to be a most harmful force on American campuses. I am willing to concede the possibility that there may, at the national level, be individuals who are solely interested in the destruction of our way of life. I am not willing, however, to say that we must sacrifice personal liberties to rid ourselves of these cancers.

In the past, I have made college records freely available to investigating officers who presented proper credentials and I have cooperated in these investigations. On reflection in the light of the above developments, I propose to withdraw myself and this institution from such cooperation, except in instances of security clearance for government positions when the individual understands he is subject to scrutiny and in investigations for specific criminal cases.

One so-called "fact" usually collected is "were you ever arrested?" While an "arrest" seems definite enough, it is often an oppressive act aimed at a minority. Arrests for "breach of the peace" are often cloaks for the arrest of people promoting unpopular ideas. Those arrests are therefore unconstitutional, since the states are subject to the First Amendment as a result of the Due Process Clause of the Fourteenth. Moreover, an arrest may be followed by an acquittal; or the case against the accused may be dismissed. Yet there are very few jurisdictions in the United States that provide procedures for "erasing" arrests. There is, moreover, no established procedure for giving an applicant a hearing on his "arrests" before they are fed into the computer and become cold, authentic "facts."

Charles Luce, when head of Bonneville Dam Authority, approved personality tests, including choices such as these:

> "I go to church every week" and "I believe in the second coming of Christ." (The latter would obviously penalize a Jew or a Moslem.)
> A. "I would like to accomplish something of great significance."
> B. "I like to kiss attractive persons of the opposite sex."
> A. "I like to praise someone I admire."
> B. "I like to be regarded as physically attractive by those of the opposite sex."
> A. "I like to keep my things neat and orderly on my desk or work space."
> B. "I like to be in love with someone of the opposite sex."

A number of federal agencies also use personality tests. One included the following choices:—my father was a good man, I am very seldom troubled by constipation, my sex life is satisfactory, evil spirits possess me at times, at times I feel like swearing, I have had very peculiar and strange experiences, I have never been in trouble because of my sex behavior, during one period when I was a youngster I engaged in petty thievery, my sleep is fitful and disturbed, I do not always tell the truth, as a youngster I was suspended from school one or more times for cutting up, everything is turning out just like the prophets of the Bible said it would.

The experts are at odds about these personality tests. These tests commonly grade a person by eight, nine, or ten traits while twenty-five thousand traits might approximate an accurate personality portrayal. Moreover, the creator of the test fashions his own neurotic world as, for example, to daydream is neurotic—the thesis that is present in one personality test.

A premise of another test is that belief in God is normal, but being *very religious* is *bad*. (Some psychiatrists affirm that "excessive religiosity" may be a symptom of mental illness.)

The most famous of these personality tests, known as MMPI, was originally designed to sort out the mentally ill. Yet some administrators have used it not for that purpose, but to determine who should be hired. MMPI has been defended by some as experimentally derived. Its defenders say that an item counts not because some clinician thought it was significant but because, in well-diagnosed groups of maladjusted or mentally ill persons, those being interviewed answered the item with an average frequency differing from the average frequency of the normative group. They point out that the item "I go to church almost every week" is counted on a scale for estimating the amount of a person's depression. Those who were depressed answered "true" with a frequency of only 20 per cent, while the normals answered "true" with a frequency of 42 per cent. So those who composed the MMPI test said that a "false" answer to this item was a count on the depression scale, although they have no idea as to why depressed people are apt to say they go to church less often than so-called normal people.

The search for the mentally ill is well-organized. So are the psychologists who clamor for a permanent place in the screening and selection of employees. And they are not resisted because the trend to conformity has made laymen less and less critical of these massive inroads on their privacy.

Personality Tests

Industry uses the personality tests to weed out those who are individualistic and assertive and to find those who tend to conform and who will therefore fit into the social climate of the industry.

A drive is on now to spot potential student protesters before they are admitted to college. A preliminary report indicates that a student is likely to be a troublemaker if he has no religious preference, if he is politically liberal rather than conservative, if he is interested in artistic pursuits and rates himself high in originality, and if he comes from a well-educated and affluent home.

Personality testing is held in awe by many people because its scales sound so definitely scientific and certain: psychopathic deviates, hypomania, schizophrenics, and so on. The psychiatrists join forces as they work on the periphery of what is "normal" and are interested in people who show "pathology." If used, these tests should cover only cases which observation, interviews, and case histories suggest are marginal. If given at all, they should be administered only by eminently qualified people; and the data collected should never enter the personnel file. The reason is plain. Someone's label "schizophrenic," "neurotic," etc., can give a person a lifetime brand, ruinous to his career, though the label may have been improperly attached to begin with. Even if it was valid at one time, the condition may have been completely cleared up. But a computer does not know any of those things.

Ideological data—like personality data—is treacherous when fed into a computer. For by its use the loyalty and security board's failure or refusal to clear a person becomes a virtually incontestable "fact." All one has to do now is to press the "subversive" button and all the names of "dangerous" people come tumbling out.

The computer has now taken place alongside the A-Bomb to mark two phenomenal revolutions in this generation. With electronics, an

idea can now be transmitted around the world
in one-seventh of a second. And so the recur-
ring question is, what ideas will be disseminated?
If they concern people, how will people be eval-
uated?

Big Brother in the form of an increasingly
powerful government and in an increasingly
powerful private sector will pile the records high
with reasons why privacy should give way to
national security, to law and order, to efficiency
of operations, to scientific advancement, and the
like. The cause of privacy will be won or lost essentially in legislative halls and in constitutional
assemblies. If it is won, this pluralistic society of
ours will experience a spiritual renewal. If it is
lost we will have written our own prescription
for mediocrity and conformity.

The tendency of these mounting invasions of
privacy is the creation of a creeping conformity
that makes us timid in our thinking at a time
when the problems which envelop us demand
bold and adventuresome attitudes.

Electronic surveillance, as well as old-fash-
ioned wire tapping, has brought Big Brother
closer to everyone and has produced a like level-

ing effect. In 1968 Congress made wiretapping and electronic surveillance lawful provided it was done with a warrant, as provided in the Fourth Amendment, issued by a judge on a showing of probable cause that certain specified crimes had been or were being committed. Exempted altogether from any supervision were national security cases where the President was given large authority to proceed against suspected spies and subversives. But the Administration soon broadened that category to include domestic groups who attempt to use unlawful means to "attack the existing structure of government." The *Wall Street Journal* sounded the alarm that such broad surveillance "could lead to the harassment of lawful dissenters." And the *New York Times,* in reply to the claim that Presidential power extends to surveillance of groups which threaten the government, observed that that was the theory behind the oppressive search warrants authorized by George III and they were the reason we got the Fourth Amendment.

The FBI and the CIA are the most notorious

offenders, but lesser lights also participate: Every phone in every federal or state agency is suspect. Every conference room in government buildings is assumed to be bugged. Every Embassy phone is an open transmitter. Certain hotels in Washington have allotments of rooms that are wired for sound and even contain two-way mirrors, so that the occupants can be taped or filmed.

It is safe to assume that in the federal capital, as well as in each state capital, there is no such thing as secret classified information.

The leveling effect of the numerous influences I have discussed is appalling. The tense and perilous times in which we live demand an invigorating dialogue. Yet we seem largely incapable of conducting one because of the growing rightist tendencies in the nation that demand conformity—or else. We are inhibited when we should be unrestrained. We are hesitant when we should be bold. It is not enough to be anticommunist. We need the irrepressible urge to rejoin the human race. We need to contribute moral and political leadership—as well

Effect of surveillence by Gov't.

as technical and financial help—to rebuilding a new world order controlled by Law rather than by Force.

This, in summary, is the mood in which America has viewed the forces of real "revolution" that have been sweeping the nation.

But what about the forces of dissent?

There are many facets to that problem, but they all lead, I think, to what has been called "the diminished man." There is more knowledge and information than ever before: the experts have so multiplied that man has a new sense of impotence; man is indeed about to be delivered over to them. Man is about to be an automaton; he is identifiable only in the computer. As a person of worth and creativity, as a being with an infinite potential, he retreats and battles the forces that make him inhuman.

The dissent we witness is a reaffirmation of faith in man; it is protest against living under rules and prejudices and attitudes that produce the extremes of wealth and poverty and that make us dedicated to the destruction of people through arms, bombs, and gases, and that pre-

pare us to think alike and be submissive objects
for the regime of the computer.

One young man wrote me his dissent in a
poem:

> Humans exist only to consume
> We the living have entered a tomb
> Machines are this world's best
> So humans are purchased to do the rest.

The dissent we witness is a protest against
the belittling of man, against his debasement,
against a society that makes "lawful" the exploitation of humans.

This period of dissent based on belief in man
will indeed be our great renaissance.

II

The Legions
of
Dissent

Students in West Germany are denouncing NATO because NATO is supposed to defend freedom, yet Greece, a cruel dictatorship, is a member. German students are inflamed at our use of napalm in Vietnam, putting to us the embarrassing question, "It's a war crime, isn't it?"

A sixteen-year-old boy in Tokyo is symbolic of the dissent that is sweeping Japan.

Japan has become identified with United States militarism; and some say Japan is now thoroughly subdued by the U. S. military approach to world problems. Japan is a huge U. S. air force base. It is also the only means by which the Seventh Fleet replenishes its supplies and is able to continue its operations in Far Eastern waters.

What worries the sixteen-year-old from Tokyo? The American fear of Peking is the major reason for our conversion of Japan into a military base. Yet neither the youth of Japan nor the older generation fears China. "We are blood brothers and have lived side by side for centuries."

Why then does Japan tolerate U. S. military bases in her country? The answer is, an overwhelming fear of Russia.

That fear by the Japanese is as senseless as our own fear of Peking. Each senseless fear feeds the other. Whatever the Japanese youth may think of Russia, he sees the American military presence in Japan as inexorably involving Japan in a conflict with Peking. Our presence there has already had dire consequences from the Japanese international viewpoint. They were pressured by us into recognizing Taipei, a step that many Japanese—young and old—deem morally wrong. For the real China is Mainland China with her 800 million people. Peking, not Taipei, is the mirror of the twenty-first century with all of its troublesome problems. The Japanese—especially the young—want to get on with those problems so that they will not fester and worsen.

The youthful dissenter in the U. S. probably

does not see the Asian situation as clearly as the Japanese dissenter unless he gets to Vietnam or nearby. Yet more and more of the youth of America are instinctively horrified at the way President Johnson avoided all constitutional procedures and slyly maneuvered us into an Asian war.

There was no national debate over a declaration of war.

The lies and half-truths that were told, and the phony excuses gradually advanced, made most Americans dubious of the integrity of our leadership.

Moreover, the lack of any apparent threat to American interests—-whether Vietnam was fascist, communist, or governed in the ancient Chinese mandarin tradition (as it was for years)— compounded the American doubts concerning our Vietnam venture. Our youth rebelled violently when Mr. Johnson used his long arm to try to get colleges to discipline the dissenters and when he turned the Selective Service System into a vindictive weapon for use against the protesters.

There is, I believe, a common suspicion

among youth around the world that the design
for living, fashioned for them by their politically
bankrupt elders, destines them either to the nuclear incinerator or to a life filled with a constant fear of it.

Various aspects of militarism have produced
kindred protests among the youth both here and
in Japan. The Japanese say that the most dread-
ful time in history was the period when only one
nation (the United States) had the atomic bomb.
Hirosima is not forgotten. To the Japanese a
sense of security came when Russia acquired the
same bomb. They reason that that created a deterrent force to the use of nuclear force by any
of the great powers.

But we know that preparedness and the arma-
ment race inevitably lead to war. Thus it ever
has been and ever will be. Armaments are no
more of a deterrent to war than the death sen-
tence is to murder. We know from our own experience that among felonies the incidence of
murder is no higher in Michigan and Minnesota
(where the death penalty was abolished years
ago) than in California and New York. Moreover, when Delaware restored the death penalty

ten years ago there was an increase, not a de-
crease, in the rate of criminal homicides.

If the war that comes is a nuclear conflict, the
end of planetary life is probable. If it is a war
with conventional weapons, bankruptcy is inevi-
table. Modern technological war is much too
expensive to fight. Vietnam has bled our country
at the rate of 2.5 billion dollars a month.

The Pentagon has a fantastic budget that en-
ables it to dream of putting down the much-
needed revolutions which will arise in Peru, in
the Philippines, and in other benighted coun-
tries.

Where is the force that will restrain the Pentagon?

Would a President dare face it down?

The strength of a center of power like the
Pentagon is measured in part by the billions of
dollars it commands. Its present budget is indeed greater than the total federal budget in
1957.

In the fiscal year beginning July 1, 1969, the
Pentagon will spend about 82 billion dollars, or
40 per cent of the federal budget. Health and
welfare will spend about 5.5 billion, or 27.2 per

cent, while community development and housing will spend 2.8 billion, or 1.4 per cent.

Beyond that inequity is the self-perpetuating
character of the Pentagon. Its officer elite is of
course subject to some controls; but those controls are mostly formal.

The Pentagon has a magnetism and energy of
its own. It exercises, moreover, a powerful impact on the public mind. A phone call or a personal visit by the Pentagon propels its numerous public spokesmen into action. On Capitol
Hill it maintains one public relations man for
every two or three Congressmen and Senators.
The mass media—essentially the voice of the
Establishment—much of the time reflects the
mood of the Pentagon and the causes which the
military-industrial complex espouses. So, we the
people are relentlessly pushed in the direction
that the Pentagon desires.

The push in that direction is increased by
powerful foreign interests. The China Lobby,
financed by the millions extorted and extracted
from America by the Kuomintang, uses vast
sums to brainwash us about Asia. The Shah of
Iran hires Madison Avenue advertising houses

control
over
Mind

[42   ]

to give a democratic luster to his military, re-
pressive dictatorship. And so it goes.

Secrecy about the crucial facts concerning
Soviet or Chinese plans is the Pentagon's most
powerful weapon. No one without that knowledge is qualified to speak. That knowledge cannot be made public, as it involves matters of national security. Senior members of the armed
services are in the know; so are their industrial
allies and their scientific allies; so are members
of the Armed Services Committee of Congress.
This is indeed a small club that holds all the se-
crets and therefore has the only qualifications to
make the crucial decisions. This kind of presti-
gious club exerts a powerful influence. Its members are so potent that they can—and do—ex-
clude critics or skeptics as security risks. So we
sail off into the nuclear sunset under orders of
those who think only in terms of death.

We have perhaps put into words the worries
and concerns of modern youth. Their wisdom
is often instinctive; or they may acquire a re-
vealing insight from gross statements made by
their elders. But part of their overwhelming fear
is the prospect of the military regime that has

ruled us since the Truman administrations and of the ominous threat that the picture holds.

Is our destiny to kill Russians? to kill Chinese?

Why cannot we work at cooperative schemes and search for the common ground binding all mankind together?

We seem to be going in the other direction. In 1970 we will spend 2 billion dollars for developing the ABM, which is more than we will allocate to community action and model cities programs combined; we will spend 2.4 billion dollars on new Navy ships, which is about twice what we will spend on education for the poor; we will spend 8 billion dollars on new weapons research, which is more than twice the current cost of the medicare program; and so on.

 Race is another source of dissent. As this is written, conflict over jobs for Blacks has erupted in Chicago, Pittsburgh, and Seattle. Blacks claim precious few jobs in ten crafts. In Chicago, they constitute 18 per cent of cement masons but only 1.7 per cent of carpenters, 0.3 per cent of pipe-fitters, and 0.2 per cent of sheet metal workers, 0.9 per cent of structural iron-workers, 2.9 per cent of plumbers.

Negroes want parity as respects human dignity—parity as respects equal justice and parity in economic opportunities. Yet, in recent years:

Two out of three Negro families have earned less than $4,000 a year, as opposed to only 27 per cent of the whites.

Only one out of five Negro families has made $6,000 or more, as opposed to one out of two white families.

The chance of a Negro, age 24, of making $3,000 or more a year is 41 per cent while the chance of a 24-year-old white is 78 per cent.

In April, 1968, only 3.5 per cent of the general population were unemployed, while for those in the slum areas it was 7 per cent, with 5.7 per cent for whites and 8.7 per cent for Negroes.

The national white unemployment rate has been about 3.1 per cent and the national Negro unemployment rate 6.7 per cent.

Police practices are anti-Negro.

Employment practices are anti-Negro.

Housing allocation is anti-Negro.

Education is anti-Negro.

The federal government, with its hundreds of federally-financed public road contracts, and its thousands of procurement contracts negotiated each year by the Pentagon and other agencies to purchase munitions, towels, stationery, pens, automobiles and the like, is admonished by Congress to make sure that the contractors for these goods make jobs available without discrimination. President Johnson gave hardly more than lip service to that mandate.

Under Richard Nixon, enforcement at first became even more lax; and then in mid-1969 the Labor Department announced that all federal contractors on projects costing more than $500,000 must submit as part of their bids "affirmative-action plans" that set specific goals for hiring Blacks and other minorities. Seven trades were selected where the new plan would be applied and Philadelphia was made the starting point. How long it will take to make this pilot project a vital force in American business is anyone's guess.

Over half of the six-and-a-half million Americans of Mexican descent in the Southwest live in poverty. Their unemployment rate is twice the national average and higher than the rate for the Blacks. The Black child in spite of the discrimination in our system completes an average of nine years of schooling. That is about two more years of schooling than the average American child of Mexican ancestry finishes. In Texas he finishes only 4.8 years on the average.

Many cities make being poor a crime. A man who wanders about looking for a job is suspect; and he and his kind are arrested by the thousands each year. The police, indeed, use "vagrancy" as the excuse for arresting people on suspicion—a wholly unconstitutional procedure in our country.

Bias against the poor is present in the usury laws and in the practices of consumer credit. The fine print in the contract often raises havoc. It may authorize not only reclaiming the TV set on default of an installment, but also reclaiming articles sold by the same merchant under a prior contract. If the dealer sells the note of the purchaser to a finance company, the latter is a so-called "holder in due course" and normally a defense of fraud, good against the dealer, is not good against the finance house. Moreover, the finance company may collect even though the dealer skips town and never delivers the articles purchased.

For the poor, the interest rates have been known to rise to 1000 per cent a year.

We got rid of our debtors' prisons in the last century. But today's garnishment proceedings are as destructive and vicious as the debtors' dungeons. Employers have often discharged workers whose wages are garnisheed; and the total runs over 250,00 a year. In many states the percentage of wages garnisheed has been so high that a man and his family are often reduced to a starvation level.

Congress in 1968 passed a law requiring full disclosure of all consumer credit charges. It also banned the discharge of employees whose wages are garnisheed; and it reduced the percentage of the weekly wage that may be garnisheed.

But the charges for consumer credit are governed almost entirely by state law; and in 1969 practically all the states (at least forty-eight out of fifty) were asked by finance company lobbies to adopt a so-called model code which increases permissible charges and makes the power of the lender even tighter over the poor. Needless to say, the finance company lobby is not recommending the introduction of neighborhood credit unions whose interest is notoriously low.

Landlord-tenant laws are also filled with bias against the poor. They have been written by the landlords' lobby, making the tenant's duty to pay rent absolute and the landlord's duty to make repairs practically non-existent. In seven or more states, laws have been passed authorizing tenants to withhold rent, placing it in escrow until the landlord makes necessary repairs and meanwhile protecting the tenant against eviction. In a few states, a receiver may be appointed to collect the rent and spend it on repairs.

Yet another major source of disaffection among our youth stems from the reckless way in which the Establishment has despoiled the earth. The matter was put by a 16-year-old boy who asked his father, "Why did you let me be born?"

His father, taken aback, asked the reason for the silly question.

The question turned out to be relevant, not silly.

At the present rate of the use of oxygen in the

air, it may not be long until there is not enough for people to breathe. The percentage of carbon dioxide in some areas is already dangerously high. Sunshine and the green leaves may not be able to make up the growing deficiency of oxygen which exists only in a thin belt around the earth.

✓ Everyone knows—including the youthful dissenters—that Lake Erie is now only a tub filled with stinking sewage and wastes.

✓ Many of our rivers are open sewers.

✓ Our estuaries are fast being either destroyed by construction projects or poisoned by pollution. Yet these estuaries are essential breeding grounds for marine life: eighty per cent of the fish, shrimp, crabs, and the like spend a critical period of their lives in some estuary.

✓ Virgin stands of timber are virtually gone.

✓ Only remnants of the once immortal redwoods remain.

✓ Pesticides have killed millions of birds, putting some of them in line for extinction.

✓ DDT, now in dangerous solution in our oceans, causes birds to produce eggs with shells too fragile for nesting. That is why the Bermuda petrel, peregrine osprey and brown pelican are doomed to extinction.

✔ DDT makes female fish sterile. Along the Atlantic coast commercial fish are reproducing at an alarmingly low rate.

✔ Hundreds of trout streams have been destroyed by highway engineers and their faulty plans.

✔ The wilderness disappears each year under the ravages of bulldozers, highway builders, and men in search of metals that will make them rich.

✔ Our coastlines are being ruined by men who search for oil yet have not mastered the technology enough to know how to protect the public interest in the process.

Youthful dissenters are not experts in these matters. But when they see all the wonders of nature being ruined they ask, "What natural law gives the Establishment the right to ruin the rivers, the lakes, the ocean, the beaches, and even the air?"

And if one tells them that the important thing is making money and increasing the Gross National Product they turn away in disgust.

Their protest is not only against what the Es-

✳ tablishment is doing to the earth but against the
callous attitude of those who claim the God-
given right to wreak that damage on the nation
without rectifying the wrong.

There are "colonies" within the United States.
West Virginia is in a sense a microcosm of such
a colony. It is partially owned and effectively
controlled by coal, power, and railroad companies, which in turn are controlled by vast financial interests of the East and Middle West.
The state legislature answers to the beck and call
of those interests. Strip mining, the curse of
several States, has easy going in West Virginia.
Black lung cancer takes an awful toll among
miners. The Establishment gave in a little and
allowed the legislature to pass a sort of a law
under which a man totally disabled from black
lung cancer gets, at the most, $2500 a year—
guaranteed to keep him at the poverty level. The
Establishment controls, of course, the agencies
and commissions that administer the welfare,
compensation, and unemployment systems of
the State. The "mother" interests that own the
wealth of West Virginia appear secure. But
under the surface there is violence boiling.

There have always been grievances and youth has been the agitator. Why then is today different? Why does dissent loom so ominously?

At the consumer credit level and at the level of housing, the deceptive practices of the Establishment have multiplied. Beyond that is the factor of communication which in the field of consumer credit implicates more and more people who, no matter how poor, with all their beings are taught to want the merchandise they see displayed. Beyond that there is another, more basic problem: that political action today is most difficult. The major parties are controlled by the Establishment and the result is a form of political bankruptcy.

An American GI in Vietnam wrote me in early 1969, stating that bald truth: "Somewhere in our history—though not intentionally—we slowly moved from a government of the people to a government of a chosen few . . . who, either by birth, family tradition or social standing—a minority possessing all the wealth and power— now . . . control the destiny of mankind."

This GI ended by saying, "You see, Mr. Douglas, the greatest cause of alienation is that my

generation has no one to turn to." And he added,
"With all the hatred and violence that exist
throughout the world it is time someone, regard-
less of personal risk, must stand up and represent the feelings, the hopes, the dreams, the vi-
sions and desires of the hundreds of thousands
of Americans who died, are dying, and will die
in the search of truth."

This young man, as a result of his experiences
in the crucible of Vietnam and in the riots at
home, has decided to enter politics and run for
office as spokesman for the poor and under-
privileged of our people.

Political action that will recast the balance
will take years.

Meanwhile, an overwhelming sense of futility
possesses the young generation. How can any
pressing, needed reforms or changes or revers-
als be achieved? There is in the end a feeling
that the individual is caught in a pot of glue and
is utterly helpless.

The truth is that a vast bureaucracy now runs
the country, irrespective of what party is in
power. The decision to spray sagebrush or mesquite trees in order to increase the production of

grass and make a cattle baron richer is that of a faceless person in some federal agency. Those who prefer horned owls or coyotes do not even have a chance to be heard.

How does one fight an entrenched farm lobby or an entrenched highway lobby?

How does one get even a thin slice of the farm benefits, that go to the rich, into the lunch boxes of the poor?

How does one give HEW, and its state counterparts, a humane approach which would rob from the bureaucrats their ability to discriminate against an illegitimate child or to conduct midnight raids without the search warrants needed before even a poor man's home may be entered by the police?

Most of the questions are beyond the reach of any remedy for the average person.

As the President of Amherst, Dr. Calvin H. Plimpton, wrote President Nixon on May 2, 1969:

"The pervasive and insistent disquiet on many campuses throughout the nation indicates that unrest results, not from a conspiracy by a few, but from a shared sense that the nation has no adequate plans for meeting the crises of our society. . . . We do not say that all of the problems faced by colleges and universities are a reflection of the malaise of the larger society. That is not true. But we do say that until political leadership addresses itself to the major problems of our society—the huge expenditure of national resources for military purposes, the inequities practiced by the present draft system, the critical needs of America's 23,000,000 poor, the unequal division of our life on racial issues—until this happens, the concern and energy of those who know the need for change will seek outlets for their frustration."

The truth is that a vast restructuring of our society is needed if remedies are to become available to the average person. Without that restructuring the good will that holds society together will be slowly dissipated.

It is that sense of futility which permeates the present series of protests and dissents. Where there is a persistent sense of futility, there is violence; and that is where we are today.

The use of violence is deep in our history.

Futility
s
Violence

Shay's Rebellion in 1786-1787 was sparked by a financial depression when land taxes were said to have become intolerable.

The Whiskey Rebellion of 1784 was a farmers' protest against a federal tax on distilled whiskeys.

Every subsequent decade showed fleeting examples of a similar kind.

In the 1930's we had "sit-down" strikes by which workers seized factories, an act which Chief Justice Hughes called "a high-handed proceeding without shadow of right."

The historic instances of violence have been episodic and have never become a constant feature of American life. Today that pattern has changed. Some demonstrations go on for months; and the protests at colleges have spread like a prairie grass fire.

We are witnessing, I think, a new American phenomenon. The two parties have become almost indistinguishable; and each is controlled by the Establishment. The modern day dissenters and protesters are functioning as the loyal opposition functions in England. They are the mounting voice of political opposition to the statuts quo, calling for revolutionary changes in our institutions.

Yet the powers-that-be faintly echo Adolf Hitler, who said in 1932:

> The streets of our country are in turmoil. The universities are filled with students rebelling and rioting.
>
> Communists are seeking to destroy our country. Russia is threatening us with her might and the republic is in danger. Yes, danger from within and without.
>
> We need law and order.

III

A Start
Towards
Reconstructing
Our Society

There always have been—and always will be—aggrieved persons. The lower their estate the more difficult it is to find a right to fit the wrong being done. Part of our problem starts at that point. In New York City a housing complaint must go to one of the nineteen bureaus that deal with those problems. It takes a sharp and energetic layman or lawyer to find the proper desk in the bureaucracy where the complaint must be lodged.

The finance company's motion for summary judgment might be defeated if the borrower had a lawyer who could show that the hidden charges, when cumulated, resulted in usurious charges.

But since no one appears in defense, a judgment is entered which is shortly used to garnishee the wages of the defendant.

The landlord's motion for eviction might be

defeated, if the tenant had a lawyer who could prove that the real basis of eviction was the tenant's activities on civil rights. Perhaps he refused to pay rent until the landlord made repairs. Normally that is no defense. The historic rule disallows the failure to make repairs as a defense to the failure to pay rent. The theory was that the duty to pay rent was dependent on the conveyance of the agreed-upon space irrespective of its condition. But in recent years lawyers have pressed the opposite position and have sometimes won. The fact is that a person with a competent lawyer has some chance; one without a lawyer has only a little chance.

The examples are as numerous as the woes and complaints of people. Most cases—civil, certainly, and many criminal ones also—are lost and neglected in the onrush of daily life for lack of any spokesmen for indigents before courts or administrative agencies.

There are at least thirty million people in this category in the country. It was to service them that the Office of Economic Opportunity established Neighborhood Legal Services in some 250 centers. In 1968 NLS processed cases involving from 750,000 to 1,000,000 people in a total of 500,000 cases. But the need is astronomical: it is estimated that the annual case-load produced by the poor alone is somewhere between five million and fifteen million.

The demand for an Ombudsman—especially in metropolitan areas—constantly recurs, and reflects a complaint of rich and poor alike that the laws have become much too complex. What is irritating to the rich is often suffocating to the poor.

Our fourth Chief Justice, John Marshall, who served from 1801 to 1834, said:

"The very essence of civil liberty certainly consists in the right of every individual to claim the protection of the laws, whenever he receives an injury."

Finding a right to correct a wrong is, however, the least of all the modern pressing problems. If poor and rich alike had lawyers to assert their claims, we would still be left with staggering problems.

The vital problems will require a great restructuring of our society. Many issues will emerge. The most immediate, though perhaps minor in the overall picture, concern two important areas.

First is the problem of reallocating our resources.

Second is the problem of creating some control or surveillance over key administrative agencies.

The most explosive issues involve the reallocation of resources. For example, the 80 billion dollar budget of the Pentagon poses inflammatory problems:

If we prepare for wars, which ones are we to fight?

Should we prepare for war or for cooperative international programs designed to prevent war and to provide suitable substitutes for it?

Should not domestic problems—racial discrimination, housing, food for the hungry, education, and the like—receive priority?

The Pentagon is ready to start constructing the ABM system and is helping scientists prepare their articles praising it. The electronics industry is firmly entrenched in the Pentagon and that industry will reap huge profits from ABM which started as a five billion dollar item,

How to restructure Society

quickly jumped to ten billion and 200 billion and even 400 billion. Congress has approved this program, though by a slim majority. The voices and pressures of the military-industrial complex seem always to suffocate the pleas of the poor as well as the pleas of those who want to be done with wars and create a cooperative world pattern for the solution of international problems.

Does social and economic justice always serve a secondary role in our society?

General David M. Shoup of the Marines has called the Pentagon and the defense industry "a powerful public opinion lobby." War has become to American civilians "an exciting adventure, a competitive game, and an escape from the dull routine of peacetime."

Our whole approach to world problems has changed. We now have what General Shoup calls the "military task force" type of diplomacy. We have eight treaties to help defend forty-eight nations if they ask us—or if we choose to intervene. Our militarism threatens to become more and more the dominant force in our lives. This is an inflammatory issue; and dissent on it will not be stilled.

The advances of technology present the problem of increasing disemployment in the private sector. We brag about our present low unemployment. But that is due to Vietnam. Without Vietnam we would have 15 per cent or more unemployment. Must we fight wars to have full employment?

Technology is in the saddle and displaces manpower. The old problem of unemployment has become the new problem of disemployment. How many of the present eighteen-year-old men and women will be permanently disemployed? Thoughts such as these fill the hearts of the young with dismay.

Automation is more complete in the petrochemical industry than in any others. From the mid-1950s on, there has been an almost steady decline in the number of "all employees" in petroleum refineries; and the same is true of "production workers"—from 147,000 in 1953 to 90,000 in 1967. An ever-increasing quantity of food and industrial goods is produced by a rapidly decreasing fraction of workers. Those displaced sometimes end up making what is called "redundant" goods, items and services of value, but quite secondary or even needless measured by basic human requirements. Those engaged in various aspects of the moon project are an illustration. Most "redundant" goods projects do not produce what the people need, e.g. more hospital beds, urban projects that replace dirty ghettos, and the like.

Some who are presently "on welfare" represent the third generation in one family on the relief rolls. There is no work available and some of these people now think they are caught as victims of a system that pays people to be poor.

Training for industrial work can take care of a portion of these people, but with the great onrush of population, private industry—unless aided by wars—will not be able to meet the employment needs.

The answer, of course, is the creation of a public sector in which people will do more than rake leaves or sell apples on street corners.

A Senate Subcommittee in 1968 proposed that 1.2 million socially useful jobs be created within the next four years in the public sector. But the proposal seemed to die there.

Where is the blueprint for a public sector?

Response

How do the disadvantaged go about the promotion of such a blueprint?

If history is a guide, the powers-that-be will not respond until there are great crises, for those in power are blind devotees to private enterprise. They accept that degree of socialism implicit in the vast subsidies to the military-industrial complex, but not that type of socialism which maintains public projects for the disemployed and the unemployed alike.

I believe it was Charles Adams who described our upside down welfare state as "socialism for the rich, free enterprise for the poor." The great welfare scandal of the age concerns the dole we give rich people. Percentage depletion for oil interests is, of course, the most notorious. But there are others. Any tax deduction is in reality a "tax expenditure," for it means that on the average the Treasury pays 52 per cent of the deduction. When we get deeply into the subject we learn that the cost of public housing for the poorest twenty per cent of the people is picayune compared to federal subsidy of the housing costs of the wealthiest twenty per cent. Thus, for 1962, Alvin Schoor in *Explorations in Social*

Policy, computed that, while we spent 870 million dollars on housing for the poor, the tax de-deductions for the top twenty per cent amounted to 1.7 billion dollars.

And the 1968 *Report of the National Commission on Civil Disorder* tells us that during a thirty-year period when the federal government was subsidizing 650,000 units of low-cost housing, it provided invisible supports, such as cheap credit and tax deductions, for the construction of more than 10 million units of middle- and upper-class housing.

The big corporate farmer who has varied business interests has a large advantage over the small farmer. The farm corporation can write off profits from non-farm enterprises against farm losses. Moreover, it gets a low capital gains rate of tax in situations such as the following: a corporation buys cattle and keeps them for several years, taking the maintenance costs as a farming loss and thereby reducing its profits from other sources. Then it sells the herd and any profit on the sale is taxed at 25 per cent.

Like examples are numerous in our tax laws, each marking a victory for some powerful lobby.

The upside down welfare state helps the rich get richer and the poor, poorer.

Other subsidies receive a greater reverence. Railroads, airlines, shipping—these are all sub-sidized; and those companies' doors are not kicked down by the police at night.

Publishers get a handsome subsidy in the form of low second-class mail rates, and publishers' rights are meticulously honored.

The subsidies given farmers are treated, not as gratuities, but as matters of entitlement.

The airspace used by radio and TV is public property. But the permittees are not charged for the use of it.

Of all these only the welfare recipient is sin-gled out for degrading supervision and control. Moreover, the poor man's welfare may be cut off without any hearing.

Mr. Justice Holmes uttered a careless dictum when he said that no one has "a constitutional right to be a policeman." The idea took hold that public employment was a privilege, not a right, and therefore conditions could be attached to it. The notion spread to public welfare: a needy person could be denied public help if he

Upside-Down
Welfare
State

did not maintain the type of abode the welfare worker approved; a person on welfare has no Fourth Amendment rights: the police are empowered to kick down the door of his home at midnight without any search warrant in order to investigate welfare violations.

But the largesse granted the radio and TV industry through permits issued may not be revoked without meticulous regard for procedural due process.

The specter of hunger that stalks the land is likely to ignite people to violent protest.

Families that make less than $3,000 a year number 13 million.

Families making less than $2,000 a year, 11 million.

Families making less than $1,000 a year, 5 million.

The condition is not peculiar to any particular State, but is nationwide. Of course, a rural family making in the neighborhood of $3,000 a year may be relatively well-off—if it has a cow, chickens, and vegetable garden. But, as the poor are driven from the land by the technological revolution in agriculture and pile up in the urban centers, these statistics on our "poor" become ominous.

The federal food program is not responsive to that growing need. It is designed by the agro-business lobby to restrict production, keep prices high, and assure profits to the producers. That lobby controls the Department of Agriculture, which as a result has made feeding the poor a subordinate and secondary function.

In one year Texas producers, who constitute .02 per cent of the Texas population, received 250 million dollars in subsidies, while the Texas poor, who constitute 28.8 per cent of the Texas population, received 7 million dollars in food assistance.

Of the thirty million poor, less than six million participate in either the national food stamp program or the surplus commodity program.

A pilot food stamp project was established in two counties of South Carolina in 1969. If a poor family makes under $360 a year, it gets food stamps free under that pilot project. A poor family making more than that but less than $1,000 a year pays for food stamps, even though the family income is not sufficient to meet family necessities. Nationwide, 17 per cent of the family budget goes for food—*on the average*. The poor who buy food stamps pay much more.

A family of four makes, say, $1,000 a year and pays $40 a month for food stamps that are worth $70. That helps; but the families still cannot afford it. Moreover, these food stamp programs do not exist as a matter of right. While the federal government pays some of their costs, the state or local government, not Washington, D. C., must initiate the food stamp program.

What do local people think of their poor? That they are a worthless lot? That hard work and industry would cure their lot? That if the local poor are well-fed they may stay; but if they are left on their own, they may emigrate and settle down in some metropolitan ghetto?

The local agencies also determine what families are "eligible" for food stamps. Their word is the law, for there are no procedures and no agency or surveillance to make sure that people are not made "ineligible" because of race, creed, or ideological views. Retailers who may receive food stamps and turn them into the local bank for cash have prescribed remedies if they are discriminated against. But the faceless, voiceless poor have no such recourse.

The hungry people have to go to the County Courthouse to be processed for "eligibility." This chore, an easy one for the sophisticated, is very nearly a barrier to the illiterate poor. Getting to town, some thirty or forty miles away, is one difficulty. Standing in line a day or more and being interrogated on personal affairs by complete strangers is another barrier. If the food program is to be effective, the agency people must take it into the hovels of the poor.

One aspect of the hunger problem concerns school lunches, originally started to help dispose of surpluses and thus protect the producers against declines in the market. They are now part of a "feeding the hungry" project. Official reports give glowing accounts of the progress made; and there has been some. But, again, whether there are school lunches in any community depends on the local school board. In schools where there are few poor students, the poor are fed. In schools where most children are poor, the school board often does not supply enough money to feed them all.

The person who must pick those allowed to eat on the limited budget is the principal. The result is that some hungry children go without lunches—80.8 per cent in Virginia, 70.4 per cent in West Virginia, 73.5 per cent in Pennsylvania, and 86.8 per cent in Maryland. Overall, the national figures show that at least two out of three needy children do not receive school lunches.

Yet, the total number of school children from families at the rock-bottom poverty level is six million.

We do not know how the two million is chosen from the six. But we do know that at times the principal disqualifies a hungry child based on his judgment of the moral character of the parents, not on the child's need.

And there is no way for the parents or the child to review that ruling of the principal.

Ninety-nine of the 253 counties in Texas took no part in the federal food program in 1968. Texas has the largest farm subsidy total in the nation but denies food aid to more poor people than any other State.

In Tuscaloosa, Alabama, forty-nine producers

divided $605,000 for not growing crops, while 21,409 poor people had no access to the federal food program.

Some States—notably New York, Louisiana, Massachusetts, and South Carolina—contribute to the cost of school lunches. But in the other States the local contribution is minor. The federal government pays about one-third of the cost of lunches (if donated food is included); the children pay the rest.

No matter what the propagandists say, hungry school children who have had lunches, in the main, either pay for the food themselves or are beneficiaries of the meager amount the federal government has put into the program.

In 1968 when Resurrection City was erected in Washington, D. C., there were Congressional hearings on this problem. An American of Mexican ancestry testified:

> We are here with brothers of other races, here in unity, in love for each other. We are all poor. We speak for the oppressed, for the hungry thousands that exist in this country, to the tortures of many kinds that have been applied to us.

We have become immune and still exist, because our pride and honesty keep us going. We are the ghosts, the sons of chiefs, gods, kings and revolutionists, here to haunt you for what is rightfully ours—the human right to exist. We come here with the same problems and the same objectives. We are a proud race of people in a racist society. We look, we feel, we eat sometimes, we sleep, we walk, we love, and we die the same.

If we are to be heard here and across the country today—it has taken a long time for you to hear the complaints up to now but don't forget we Mexican-American people have waited four hundred years to be heard—if you intend to help us, do so now. Don't pass the buck or stall any longer.

The problem of hunger—like the ghetto problem and the racial problem—has festered for years. The Puritan ethic that hard work and thrift will take anyone to the top has conditioned much of our thinking and has made us slow to deal with the problems of hunger and ghettos. Those problems suddenly loom large and ominous because of the mounting population and the growing dependence of people on government.

Property has assumed a different form. To the average man it is no longer cows, horses, chickens, and a plot of land. It is government largesse—farm subsidies, social security, veterans' benefits, unemployment insurance, old-age pensions, medicare, and the like. Even business has a towering stake in government largesse, as witness the $80 billion dollar budget of the Pentagon.

The political struggles ahead are for increasing shares of government largesse. The opposed forces are numerous. On one side are powerful lobbies such as the industrial-military complex, the agro-business lobby, and the highway lobby. These have powerful spokesmen. The poor, the unemployed, and the disemployed are opposed —and they are not well organized.

The use of violence as an instrument of persuasion is therefore inviting and seems to the discontented to be the only effective protest.

Our second great task is to control the American bureaucracy. As the problems of the nation and the states multiplied, the laws became more prolix and the discretion granted the administrators became greater and greater. Licenses or permits are issued if the agency deems it to be "in the public interest." Management of national forests and national parks is left to federal agencies which in turn promulgate regulations governing the use of these properties but seldom allow a public voice to be heard against any plan of the agency.

The examples are legion and they cover a wide range of subjects from food stamps, to highway locations, to spraying of forests or grasslands to eliminate certain species of trees or shrubs, to the location of missile bases, to the disposal of sewage or industrial wastes, to the granting of off-shore oil leases.

Corporate interests, as well as poor people— unemployed people as well as the average member of this affluent society—are affected by these broad generalized grants of authority to administrative agencies. The corporate interests have been largely taken care of by highly qualified lawyers acting in individual cases and by Bar Associations proposing procedural reforms that define, for example, the "aggrieved" persons who have standing to object to agency

orders or decisions. But the voices of the mass
of people are not heard; and the administrative
agencies largely have their own way.

Moreover, the Establishment controls those
agencies. That control does not come from cor-
rupt practices or from venality. It results from
close alliances made out of working relations,
from memberships in the same or similar clubs,
from the warp and woof of social relations, and
from the prospects offered the administrator for
work in the ranks of the Establishment, *if* he is
the right and proper man. The administrative
office is indeed the staging ground where men
are trained and culled and finally chosen to the
high salaried posts in the Establishment that
carry many desirable fringe benefits. The New
Dealers mostly ended up there. Under Lyndon
Johnson there was lively competition for administrative men who would in two years have
made a million working for the Establishment.
That is a powerful influence among many agencies; and it results in those who have agency
discretion exercising it for the benefit of those
who run the corporation state. And those people
are by and large the exploiters.

Estab. relationships

Pollution

Anyone who opposes one of those federal agencies whose decision may destroy a lake or river or mountain knows something about the feeling of futility that is abroad in the land.

Agencies—notably the Forest Service and Bureau of Land Management—spray public lands to get rid of a shrub like the sagebrush or a tree like the mesquite. It is said that riddance of those species increases the supply of grass. The driving force behind the scene is the cattle baron who grazes his stock on public lands.

Neither his request for spraying nor the agency's decision to authorize it is put down for a hearing. Though Rachel Carson's *Silent Spring* has been out some years and though the dangers of pesticides are increasingly known, the agency has no "control" plot where the precise effect of the particular herbicide on our ecology has been studied. The agency, in other words, goes at the problem blindly. It will learn what damage the spray does only years after the spraying has been completed. Moreover, the public is not allowed to protest at a hearing or tender expert testimony as to what this particular spray will do to the environment. This is public land. Why should not members of the public have a right to be heard? No satisfactory answer has been given—only the desire of the agency to be rid of all outside interference.

Once in a blue moon a hearing is held. Early in 1969 the Forest Service's proposal to spray the Dry Fork in the Big Horn National Forest in Wyoming was put down for a hearing so that Norma Ketchum—but no other member of the public—could be heard. Why only that one lady? Senator Gale McGee at her request spoke to the Forest Service about the project. Because of his political pressure, this one lady was heard.

But spraying regularly takes place with no one being heard.

Private persons, as well as government agencies, do this spraying. Why should a private owner not be required to put his spraying project down for a public hearing? He may own the mesquite trees; but he does not own the wildlife that comes and goes across his property.

In 1968 and 1969 great stretches of the Sonora Desert in Arizona were sprayed to kill mesquite in order to help the cattlemen. Such a large number of kangaroo rats and other rodents were killed that the horned owls left the country for lack of food.

Does not the horned owl have value to the environment?

I remember an alpine meadow in Wyoming where willows lined a clear, cold brook. Moose browsed the willow. Beaver came and made a dam which in time created a lovely pond which produced eastern brook trout up to five pounds. A cattle baron said that sagebrush was killing the grass. So the Forest Service sprayed the entire area. It killed the sagebrush and the willow too. The moose disappeared and so did the beaver. In time the dam washed out and the pond was drained. Ten years later some of the willow was still killed out; the beaver never returned; nor did the moose.

Why should a thing of beauty that hundreds of people enjoy be destroyed to line the pockets of one cattle baron?

The agency decision that destroys the environment may be the cutting of a virgin stand of timber or the construction of a road up a wilderness valley. Hundreds of actions of this kind take place every year; and it is the unusual case on which the public is heard.

In 1961-1962 the Forest Service made plans to build a road up the beautiful Minam River in Oregon—one of the few roadless valleys in the State. It is choice wilderness—delicate in structure, sparse in timber, and filled with game. We who knew the Minam pleaded against the road. The excuse was cutting timber—a poor excuse because of the thin stand. The real reason was road building on which the lumber company would make a million dollars. The road would be permanent, bringing automobiles in by the thousands and making a shambles of the Minam.

We spoke to Senator Wayne Morse about the problem and he called over Orville Freeman, Secretary of Agriculture, the agency that supervises the Forest Service. Morse pounded the table and demanded a public hearing. One was reluctantly given. Dozens of people appeared on the designated day in La Grande, Oregon, not a blessed one speaking in favor of the plan. Public opposition was so great that the plan was suffocated.

Why should not the public be heard whenever an agency decides to take action that will or may despoil the environment?

The design of a highway, as well as its location, may be ruinous to economic, aesthetic, scenic, recreational, or health interests.

By highway design and construction the Bureau of Public Roads has ruined fifty trout streams in the Pacific Northwest. Gravel and rocks have been dumped in the streams, making the water too fast for trout or salmon. Rivers have been dredged, with the result that they have become sterile sluiceways.

Why should not the public be allowed to speak before damage of that character is done?

Racial problems often are the key to a freeway crisis. In Washington, D. C., the pressure from the Establishment was so great on the planners that the natural corridor for the freeway was abandoned and the freeway laid out so it would roar through the Black community. That experience was not unique. Many urban areas have felt the same discrimination. The Blacks—having no voice in the decision—rise up in protest, some reacting violently.

Why should not all people—Blacks as well as
Whites—be allowed to appear, by right, before
a tribunal that is impartial and not a stooge
for the powerful Highway Lobby, to air their
complaints and state their views?

Why should any special interest be allowed
to relocate a freeway merely to serve its private
purposes?

The Highway Lobby makes the Bureau of
Public Roads almost king. In 1968, when Alan
Boyd proposed hearing procedures before fed-
erally supported highways were either *located*
or *designed,* public hearings on the proposed
regulations were held. Every one of our fifty
governors appeared or sent word *opposing* the
regulations. Why? Because the national highway lobby and the state highway departments
have such a close working partnership that
nothing should be done to disrupt it. That means
that they think that individuals should have no
voice in planning. Yet the location of a highway
may: (a) ruin a park, as those in Washington,
D.C. know from the repeated threats to Glover
Archbold Park; (b) ruin the scenic values of a
river; (c) needlessly divide a unitary suburban

area into separate entities; (d) ruin a trout stream (as some fifty highways have done in the Pacific Northwest); (e) have an ugly racial overtone, as where a freeway is diverted by the Bureau from a white area and sent roaring through the middle of a Black section.

The values at stake are both aesthetic and spiritual, social and economic; and they bear heavily on human dignity and responsibility. Is a faceless bureaucrat to tell us what is beautiful? Whether a particular type of highway is more socially desirable than the country's best trout stream? Whether a particularly described highway is more desirable than a wilderness park? Whether the Blacks should be sent scurrying so that the whites can live in peace and quiet? Where do the Blacks go but into more crowded neighboring slums, as there are no suburban slums yet created?

Offshore leasing of oil lands has become another explosive issue. Offshore oil wells may result in leakages that ruin a vast stretch of beaches, as recently happened at Santa Barbara. Conservationists, if heard, could have built a strong case against the permits. Without

any hearings, Secretary of the Interior Udall
was allowed to do the bidding of the oil companies and knuckle under to the pressure of
President Johnson to start more money coming
into the federal treasury to wage war in Vietnam. The result was that the beaches of Santa
Barbara were ruined by one man's *ipse dixit*.

The tragedies that are happening to our environment as a result of agency actions are too
numerous to list. They reach into every State
and mount in intensity as our resources dimin-
ish.

People march and protest but they are not
heard.

As a result, Congressman Richard L. Ot-
tinger of New York has recently proposed that
a National Council on the Environment be
created and granted power to stay impending
agency action that may despoil the natural resources and to carry the controversy into the
courts or before Congress, if necessary.

Violence has no constitutional sanction; and
every government from the beginning has moved
against it.

But where grievances pile high and most of the

elected spokesmen represent the Establishment, violence may be the only effective response.

In some parts of the world the choice is between peaceful revolution and violent revolution to get rid of an unbearable yoke on the backs of people, either religious, military, or economic. The Melville account from Guatemala is in point. Thomas R. Melville and Arthur Melville are two Maryknoll Fathers and Marian P. Bradford, a nun, who later married Thomas.

These three worked primarily among the Indians who make up about 56 per cent of the population of Guatemala. They saw the status quo, solidly aligned against the Indians, being financed by our Alliance For Progress and endowed with secret intelligence service to ferret out all "social disturbers." Between 1966 and 1967 they saw more than 2800 intellectuals, students, labor leaders, and peasants assassinated by right-wing groups because they were trying to combat the ills of Guatemalan society. Men trying to organize unions were shot, as were men trying to form cooperatives. The Melvilles helped the Indians get a truck to transport

* Violence as a response

lime from the hills to the processing plant, an operation historically performed by Indians who carried one hundred-pound packs on their backs. A truck would increase the production of the Indians and help raise their standard of living. But the powers-that-be ran this truck off the road into a deep canyon and did everything else possible to defeat this slight change in the habits of the Indians.

And so the Indians faced the issue of whether the use of violence in self-defense was justified. The simple question they asked their priests was whether they would go to hell if they used violence.

The Melvilles said:

> Having come to the conclusion that the actual state of violence, composed of the malnutrition, ignorance, sickness and hunger of the vast majority of the Guatemalan population, is the direct result of a capitalistic system that makes the defenseless Indian compete against the powerful and well-armed landowner, my brother and I decided not to be silent accomplices of the mass murder that this system generates.
>
> We began teaching the Indians that no one will defend their rights if they do not defend them

themselves. If the government and oligarchy are using arms to maintain them in their position of misery, then they have the obligation to take up arms and defend their God-given right to be men.

Their final conclusion was "Our response to the present situation is not because we have read either Marx or Lenin, but because we have read the New Testament."

That is also what Dom Helder Camara, Archbishop of Recife, Brazil, was telling the world in 1969. "My vocation," he said, "is to argue, argue, argue for moral pressure upon the lords." The "lords" are the "slavemasters"—the Establishment in Brazil and the United States, now dedicated to crushing any move towards violent upheaval. Though violence is not open to Archbishop Camara, he said, "I respect the option for violence."

Guatemala and Brazil are token feudal situations characteristic of the whole world. They represent a status quo that must be abolished.

We of the United States are not in that category. But the risk of violence is a continuing one in our own society, because the oncoming generation has two deep-seated convictions:

Reason for Violence

First   The welfare program works in reverse by syphoning off billions of dollars to the rich and leaving millions of people hungry and other millions feeling the sting of discrimination.

Second   The special interests that control government use its powers to favor themselves and to perpetuate regimes of oppression, exploitation, and discrimination against the many.

There are only two choices: A police state in which all dissent is suppressed or rigidly controlled; or a society where law is responsive to human needs.

If society is to be responsive to human needs, a vast restructuring of our laws is essential.

Realization of this need means adults must awaken to the urgency of the young people's unrest—in other words there must be created an adult unrest against the inequities and injustices in the present system. If the government is in jeopardy, it is not because we are unable to cope with revolutionary situations. Jeopardy means that either the leaders or the people do not realize they have all the tools required to make the revolution come true. The tools and the oppor-

Gov't in
Jeopardy

[92   ]

tunity exist. Only the moral imagination is miss-
ing.

If the budget of the Pentagon were reduced
from 80 billion dollars to 20 billion it would
still be over twice as large as that of any other
agency of government. Starting with vast reduc-
tions in its budget, we must make the Pentagon
totally subordinate in our lives.

The poor and disadvantaged must have lawyers to represent them in the normal civil problems that now haunt them.

Laws must be revised so as to eliminate their
present bias against the poor. Neighborhood
credit unions would be vastly superior to the
finance companies with their record of anguished
garnishments.

Hearings must be made available so that the
important decisions of federal agencies may be
exposed to public criticism before they are put
into effect.

The food program must be drastically revised
so that its primary purpose is to feed the hungry
rather than to make the corporate farmer rich.

A public sector for employment must be cre-

ated that extends to meaningful and valuable
work. It must include many arts and crafts, the
theatre, industries; training of psychiatric and
social workers, and specialists in the whole
gamut of human interest.

The universities should be completely freed
from CIA and from Pentagon control, through
grants of money or otherwise. Faculties and
students should have the basic controls so that
the university will be a revolutionary force that
helps shape the restructuring of society. A university should not be an adjunct of business, nor
of the military, nor of government. Its curriculum should teach change, not the status quo.
Then, the dialogue between the people and the
powers-that-be can start; and it may possibly
keep us all from being victims of the corporate
state.

The constitutional battle of the Blacks has
been won, but equality of opportunity has, in
practice, not yet been achieved. There are many,
many steps still necessary. The secret is continuous progress.

Whatever the problem, those who see no escape are hopelessly embittered. A minimum necessity is measurable change.

George III was the symbol against which our Founders made a revolution now considered bright and glorious. George III had not crossed the seas to fasten a foreign yoke on us. George III and his dynasty had established and nurtured us and all that he did was by no means oppressive. But a vast restructuring of laws and institutions was necessary if the people were to be content. That restructuring was not forthcoming and there was revolution.

We must realize that today's Establishment is the new George III. Whether it will continue to adhere to his tactics, we do not know. If it does, the redress, honored in tradition, is also revolution.

Poets and authors have told us that our society has been surfeited with goods, that our people are mostly well-fed, that marketing and advertising devices have put into our hands all manner and form of gadgets to meet any whim, but that we are unhappy and not free.

The young generation sees this more clearly

than their parents do. The youngsters who rise up in protest have not formulated a program for action. Few want to destroy the system. The aim of most of them is to regain the freedom of choice that their ancestors lost, to be free, to be masters of their destiny.

We know by now that technology can be toxic as well as tonic. We know by now that if we make technology the predestined force in our lives, man will walk to the measure of its demands. We know how leveling that influence can be, how easy it is to computerize man and make him a servile thing in a vast industrial complex.

This means we must subject the machine—technology—to control and cease despoiling the earth and filling people with goodies merely to make money. The search of the young today is more specific than the ancient search for the Holy Grail. The search of the youth today is for ways and means to make the machine—and the vast bureaucracy of the corporation state and of government that runs that machine—the servant of man.

That is the revolution that is coming.

That revolution—now that the people hold the residual powers of government—need not be a repetition of 1776. It could be a revolution in the nature of an explosive political regeneration. It depends on how wise the Establishment is. If, with its stockpile of arms, it resolves to suppress the dissenters, America will face, I fear, an awful ordeal.

ABOUT THE AUTHOR

WILLIAM O. DOUGLAS was a practicing lawyer in New York City and the state of Washington, a law professor at Columbia and Yale Universities; and Chairman of the Securities and Exchange Commission. He has been a member of the Supreme Court since 1939. Justice Douglas' hobbies include hiking, conservation, foreign travel and exploration. He is the author of thirty books, including: *Towards a Global Federalism, Russian Journey, Beyond the High Himalayas, Almanac of Liberty, Farewell to Texas.* The present book, *Points of Rebellion,* is the first of three volumes dealing with dissent and rebellion. The second, *International Dissent,* will deal with world problems, and the third book, *A Hemispheric Co-op,* will consider the special problems of Latin America.

A free catalogue of VINTAGE BOOKS *will be sent at your request. Write to* Vintage Books, 457 Madison Avenue, New York, New York 10022.

VINTAGE HISTORY—AMERICAN

A free catalogue of VINTAGE BOOKS *will be sent at your request. Write to* Vintage Books, 457 Madison Avenue, New York, New York 10022.

A free catalogue of VINTAGE BOOKS *will be sent at your request. Write to* Vintage Books, 457 Madison Avenue, New York, New York 10022.

VINTAGE WORKS OF SCIENCE
AND PSYCHOLOGY

A free catalogue of VINTAGE BOOKS *will be sent at your request. Write to* Vintage Books, 457 Madison Avenue, New York, New York 10022.

A free catalogue of VINTAGE BOOKS *will be sent at your request. Write to* Vintage Books, 457 Madison Avenue, New York, New York 10022.

A free catalogue of VINTAGE BOOKS *will be sent at your request. Write to* Vintage Books, 457 Madison Avenue, New York, New York 10022.